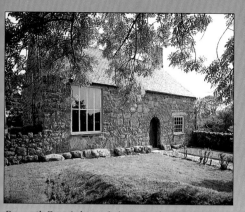

Pennarth Fawr is located about 5 miles (8km) west of Criccieth. It lies on a minor road, approximately ½ mile (0.8km) north of the A497. OS 1:50,000 map sheet 123 (NGR SH419376).

St Cybi's Well lies about 5 miles north-west of Criccieth. It is situated on the north side of the village of Llangybi, which is on a minor road approximately 1½ miles (2.4km) north of the B4354. OS 1:50,000 map sheet 123 (NGR SH427412).

Criccieth is a holiday resort on the south coast of the Lleyn Peninsula, Gwynedd. It lies on the A497 road between Porthmadog and Pwllheli, which is a bus route. OS 1:50,000 map sheet 123/124 (NGR SH500377).

The fair wall that you see, and the bright fortress on the cliftop, and the red stone on the edge of a field, that is Criccieth, a fine old building. And the old battle-scarred warrior is Sir Hywel with his wife, and her handmaidens sewing silk in the sunlight by a glass window. The splendid standard that you see is Sir Hywel's pennoncel with its three fleurs-de-lis on a black background.

Iolo Goch

Criccieth Castle

History

The great seal [cast], 1205-06, of Llywelyn ab Iorwerth (By permission of the National Museum of Wales).

C RICCIETH CASTLE is situated on a rocky, coastal promontory within the old Welsh commote of Eifionydd in the north-eastern corner of Cardigan Bay. This commote, together with that of Ardudwy, to the south-east, comprised the district or *cantref* of Dunoding. With the passage of time, and divided from one another by the estuary of the Traeth Mawr, the two commotes developed their own distinctive identities.

The principal route across Eifionydd was the old road running south from the Roman fort of *Segontium* on the outskirts of Caernarfon. The administrative centre, *maerdref*, of the commote was established at Dolbenmaen, to the north of Criccieth, at a ford where this road crossed the Afon Dwyfor. This later became the site of a small earth and timber castle, the mound or *motte* of which survives to the present day. Although probably built by the Normans at the end of the eleventh century, the castle soon fell into Welsh hands and may have continued in occupation until the 1230s when Llywelyn ab Iorwerth (Llywelyn the Great) transferred the commotal centre to Criccieth, where he built the present castle.

The castle mound or motte *at Dolbenmaen.*

The Castle of the Welsh Princes

I N 1239 DAFYDD, Llywelyn ab Iorwerth's legitimate son, imprisoned his half-brother, Gruffudd, and Gruffudd's son, Owain, at Criccieth and this is probably the earliest reference to a castle on this site. In August

A section of text from the Brut y Tywysogyon *(Chronicle of the Princes) which refers to Dafydd imprisoning Gruffudd and his son at Criccieth in 1239 (By courtesy of the National Library of Wales, Peniarth Ms. 19, column 639).*

1241, a year after his father's death, Dafydd suffered a humiliating defeat at the hands of Henry III. As one of the terms of the resulting settlement, he was forced to hand over his prisoners to the English king who claimed the right to arbitrate, if he so wished, over Gruffudd's claim to a share of the principality of Gwynedd. In the event, Gruffudd, still a prisoner, fell to his death whilst trying to escape from the Tower of London three years later.

King Henry III (1207-72), a detail from his gilt-bronze tomb effigy in Westminster Abbey. During the king's long reign, much energy was devoted to curbing the expansionist policies of Llywelyn ab Iorwerth and Llywelyn ap Gruffudd. He was forced to acknowledge the latter as prince of Wales under the Treaty of Montgomery in 1267 (By courtesy of the Dean and Chapter of Westminster).

Gruffudd falling to his death whilst attempting to escape from the Tower of London in 1244, as depicted by the contemporary chronicler, Matthew Paris (By permission of the British Library, Royal Ms. 14 C VII, f.136).

during the first forty years of the thirteenth century. It was left to Dafydd's nephew, Gruffudd's son, Llywelyn, to pursue the lengthy task of reasserting the authority of the house of Gwynedd, culminating, in 1267, in the Treaty of Montgomery and royal recognition of Llywelyn as prince of Wales.

Criccieth is again referred to as a prison in 1259. One of Llywelyn's allies in south-west Wales, Maredudd ap Rhys Gryg, having broken with Llywelyn in 1258 and sided with the English, was subsequently captured and brought to trial on 28 May 1259. Convicted of treason by his peers, he was imprisoned in Criccieth Castle until Christmas of that year, when he was released upon the forfeiture of land and having given his son as a pledge of future obedience.

A letter, apparently dated 26 February 1274 and sent by Llywelyn to Edward I from Criccieth, indicates that the prince's itinerant court was then staying in Criccieth, presumably at the castle.

By the time of his death in 1246, Dafydd had lost all the power and territorial gains that his father had acquired and consolidated

Letter sent by Llywelyn in 1274 from Criccieth to King Edward I (Copyright: Public Record Office, SC 1/19/32).

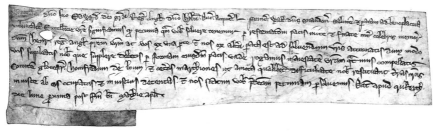

Repairs and Remodelling under King Edward I

THE CASTLE had been in unbroken Welsh possession for over forty years when, on Palm Sunday 1282, Llywelyn ap Gruffudd's brother, Dafydd, mounted an attack on Hawarden castle, precipitating the second war between Edward I and Llywelyn. By the end of the year Llywelyn was dead, struck down in a skirmish with English troops near Builth. Dolwyddelan Castle, in the heart of

King Edward I with his senior churchmen, from a manuscript of about 1285 (By permission of the British Library, Cotton Vitellius Ms. A XIII, f.6v)

Dolwyddelan Castle from the west.

English borough at Criccieth. On 23 December of the same year he appointed Sir William Leyburn as the new constable of the castle at an annual fee of £100, out of which he had to maintain a garrison of thirty men.

Late thirteenth-century seal of the borough of Criccieth (By kind permission of the Trustees of the British Museum).

Snowdonia, fell to the English on 18 January 1283, and it may have been a detachment of troops from there which then marched against Criccieth. There are no surviving records relating to the capture of the castle, but it was in English hands by 14 March, from which date Henry of Greenford received wages as its constable.

Edward I visited the castle on a number of occasions in 1283 and 1284 and, by a charter dated 22 November 1284, he established a free

Letter sent by Edward I on 15 August 1283 from Criccieth to his clerks William de Perton and John de Maidenstan (Copyright: Public Record Office, SC 1/45/24).

The borough of Criccieth was always small, and along with the similarly-sized borough of Harlech, it seems never to have had stone walls, its inhabitants seeking the protection of the castle in times of trouble. Under the terms of the charter the constable of the castle also acted as mayor of the borough.

It is difficult to estimate Edward I's total expenditure on building works at the castle between 1283 and 1292. Criccieth is listed as one of the castles at which the keeper of the Wardrobe laid out over £9,400 for works in the years 1283 and 1284. The expenditure at Criccieth, and the nature of the works there, are not specified. However, we do know that a total of £353 was spent on building works at the castle between 1285 and 1292 and it is thought that the overall expenditure for the entire period (1283-92) might have been in the region of £500. Having arrived at this figure, there remains the problem of establishing which parts of the castle it was spent upon and this is discussed on pp.14-5.

In 1294 Madog ap Llywelyn, a distant cousin of Llywelyn ap Gruffudd, led a Welsh rising against the English which rapidly spread throughout Wales. Caernarfon town and castle were overrun and set on fire, and Roger de Pulesdon, the Sheriff of Anglesey, was killed. The castles of Criccieth, nearby Harlech, and Aberystwyth were beseiged and throughout the winter they had to rely on their coastal positions and sea-borne communications for survival. The garrison at

Criccieth Castle from the east. Its coastal location enabled the garrison to hold out in the siege of 1294-95.

The coat of arms of Sir William Leyburn.

Below: *Harlech Castle from the east.*
Bottom: *Aberystwyth Castle, looking south from the main gatehouse.*

Criccieth, consisted of 29 men under the command of Sir William Leyburn, along with 41 people from the town who had sought refuge within the castle. It held out until the beginning of the following April when the castle was relieved and supplies were brought in by sea from Ireland.

In 1296 the castle reverted to its earlier role as a prison, with the arrival of prisoners from King Edward's Scottish war in June of that year. There is a further reference to the castle serving as a prison in 1319, and prisoners appear to have been kept in the castle almost until its destruction by Owain Glyndŵr in 1404.

The Fourteenth Century

OVER £250 was spent on the castle during the reign of Edward II (1307-27) and we are somewhat better informed about how that money was used. Several towers are named, although in some cases it is difficult to identify these with surviving towers.

In 1310-11, £12 5s. 2d. was spent on 'making a tower called Leyburn Tower by taskwork'. This tower is probably named after Sir William Leyburn, the above-mentioned second constable of the castle, but the sum recorded is insufficient for the construction of a new tower, and must relate merely to repairing an existing tower. The roof of the 'upper step of the Mountfort Tower' was repaired in 1312-13. This tower may well have been named after Llywelyn ap Gruffudd's wife, Eleanor de Montfort, the daughter of Simon de Montfort.

Effigy of King Edward II (1284-1327) from his tomb at Gloucester Cathedral (By courtesy of the National Portrait Gallery).

These named towers were probably the south-east and south-west towers, but it is impossible to tell which was which.

There are a number of references to what must be the final heightening of the gatehouse. In 1315, 29s. 8d. was spent on raising the wall of the 'twin' tower and this work was completed in the following year with the further expenditure of £22 2s. 7d. This latter sum was apportioned into £4 18s. 7d. for raising the masonry of the 'Cistern Tower' and laying new joists on it; £14 for cutting and preparing the timber work, and £3 4s. 0d. for the lead roof. The 'twin' and 'Cistern' towers must, therefore, be those of the inner gatehouse with the 'Cistern Tower' taking its name from the water cistern in the gateway passage (pp.21-2).

Between 7 February and 1 May 1317 a sum of 16s. 10d. was spent on the wages of masons making a stone wall below the posts and side walls of the King's Hall. At the same time boards, lintels, posts and sills were being purchased, and carpenters paid for repairing the hall. More repairs were undertaken in 1320, when a carpenter was employed to repair that end of the hall nearest to the castle gate. The King's Hall, which first appears in the accounts in 1296, appears to have been a timber-framed structure built against the inner face of the north-western stretch of the inner curtain wall.

A mid thirteenth-century illustration showing building construction, from a drawing by Matthew Paris (By permission of the British Library, Cotton Nero Ms. D I, f.23v).

A survey of the castle in 1321 reported that the gates were very weak, and much of the timber of the castle rotting, because of the poor state of the lead roofs. A further survey in 1343, when the castle came into the hands of Prince Edward, the Black Prince, estimated that £96 needed to be spent on repairs. The roof of the great hall and those of the Great Tower, Le Gynnetour, the Layburn (*sic*) Tower, and Le Sister Tour were all in need of repair. Le Sister Tour is presumably the Cistern Tower mentioned in 1316, and the Layburn (*sic*) Tower has also been mentioned before. Le Gynnetour, or Engine Tower, probably refers to the north tower. It is interesting to note in this connection that an inventory of the armament in the castle, undertaken at the same time, mentions a rotten *springald* (catapult), which might well have been the type of weapon mounted on this tower.

The coat of arms of Sir Hywel ap Gruffudd.

Section from a mid sixteenth-century copy of Iolo Goch's poem, Sir Hywel of the Axe. *It records his heroic deeds and mentions Criccieth Castle (By courtesy of Cardiff Central Library, MS. 5.167).*

A gilt-bronze effigy of Edward, prince of Wales, the Black Prince (1330-76) in Canterbury Cathedral (By courtesy of the Conway Library, Courtauld Institute of Art).

In about 1359 the Black Prince appointed Sir Hywel ap Gruffudd as Criccieth's first Welsh constable. Syr Hywel y Fwyall (Sir Howel of the Battle-axe), as he was also known, had campaigned in France with Edward III and the prince, and served with distinction at the battles of Crécy and Poitiers. As a local man, he returned in honour with his heroic deeds being commemorated in Iolo Goch's poem, *Sir Hywel of the Axe*. He remained constable of the castle until his death in about 1381 and this period has been regarded as the heyday of Criccieth.

7

Owain Glyndŵr and the Fall of the Castle

GROWING UNREST in Wales during the last quarter of the fourteenth century finally erupted into open revolt in 1400, when Owain Glyndŵr and his followers attacked some English boroughs in north-east Wales. The garrison at Criccieth was strengthened, and in 1402-03 the constable, Roger Acton, had 6 men-at-arms and 50 archers under his command at an annual cost of £416 14s. 2d.

By the end of 1403 much of the country was under Owain's control and the English garrisons were besieged at a number of castles, including Criccieth and the key castles of Harlech and Aberystwyth.

Eventually, deprived of seaborne provisions by a French fleet active in the Irish Sea in support of Owain, Harlech and Aberystwyth castles surrendered in the spring of 1404. Criccieth seems to have capitulated at about the same time and both the castle and borough were destroyed. Layers of burnt material, probably dating to this destruction,

Criccieth Castle as painted by J.M.W. Turner sometime between 1835-36. In the foreground shipwrecked sailors are engaged in salvage under the supervision of coastguard officers (By kind permission of the Trustees of the British Museum).

were found during the excavation of the gatehouse, the south-east and south-west towers, and the walls of these last two were burnt red.

The seal of Owain Glyndŵr. Criccieth Castle was besieged by the forces of Glyndŵr over the winter of 1403-04. Cut off from relief, the garrison eventually surrendered soon after the fall of nearby Harlech. The castle appears to have been burnt by the rebels, never again to be rebuilt (by permission of the National Museum of Wales).

Criccieth Castle was never rebuilt, and it was some years before the borough gradually recovered, although with the loss of the castle it was no longer a garrison borough and henceforth it became wholly Welsh. John Leland, who travelled throughout England and Wales between 1535 and 1545, described the town as follows: 'At Crikith be a 2. or 3. poore houses, and there is a smaule rylle. There hath beene a franchisid toune, now clene decayed'.

Repair and Excavation

THE CASTLE remained in the possession of the Crown until 1858 when the ruins were sold to W. Ormsby Gore M.P. Minor repairs appear to have been carried out in the late nineteenth century and again shortly before Lord Harlech placed the castle in State care in 1933.

Very little of the masonry of the outer ward and only part of the south-east tower were visible when work started on preserving the fabric of the castle. Hand-in-hand with the consolidation of the upstanding masonry, B.H. St J. O'Neil supervised the excavation of the buried remains until the full extent of the castle was revealed as we see it today. In 1944 he published a detailed study of the castle, including a report on his excavations, in the journal *Archaeologia Cambrensis* and this has formed the basis of the present guide (p.10).

The site is now maintained by Cadw: Welsh Historic Monuments, on behalf of the Secretary of State for Wales.

Building Sequence and Dating

Problems of Dating

I N RECENT YEARS the dating of Criccieth Castle has been the subject of a lively controversy, the debate centring on the difficulty of reconciling the surviving structural remains with the sums of money known to have been spent on the castle during the reigns of Edward I and his son, Edward II.

B.J. St J. O'Neil, in his detailed description of the castle, used the different types of building stone and mortar to distinguish the various periods in its history. On this basis he identified the inner and outer rings of masonry as belonging to two separate phases, both dated to the pre-Edwardian, Welsh, castle.

Subsequent research into contemporary documents has shown that both Edward I and Edward II spent considerably more on the castle than was thought when O'Neil wrote his original report. This led C.N. Johns, when revising the official guidebook in 1970, to suggest that the inner ring was built by Edward I, as a secondary feature within an earlier Welsh castle. The controversy which followed centred on the difficulty of reconciling this interpretation with surviving structural evidence.

There is, perhaps, no easy solution to this problem, particularly as the outer ward of the castle is now so ruinous. The interpretation which follows returns to O'Neil's original view that much of the surviving masonry is of the Welsh period, but suggests ways in which the fairly substantial sums of money provided by the English kings might have been spent.

Archaeologia Cambrensis

VOL. XCVIII. PART I. 1944.

CRICCIETH CASTLE, CAERNARVONSHIRE.
By B. H. St. J. O'NEIL, F.S.A.

A. HISTORY.

THE cantref of Dunoding, named after Dunod (Latin *Donatus*), one of the sons of Cunedda, comprised two commotes, Arduddwy to the south, now in northern Merioneth, and Eifionydd, named after Dunod's son, Eifion, to the north and west. Between the two lay Y Traeth Mawr (the Great Sand), a great natural barrier, so that it is not surprising to learn of the divergence in history of the two commotes.

Eifionydd, within which lies Criccieth, and which stretched from the Traeth on the east to the Afon Erch on the west, and was bounded on the south by the sea and on the north by the high mountains, according to the earliest records was ruled by a local dynasty, tracing its origin to Dunod. These rulers appear to have held their own until well on into the tenth century (c. A.D. 930), but the commote then fell under the domination of Gwynedd, its more powerful neighbour to the north.

The residence of the local chieftain in these early times, whether independent or under the rule of Gwynedd, is unknown, but it is unlikely to have been far from the important route, which passed through the commote between Caernarvon and Arduddwy. This route undoubtedly crossed the Afon Dwyfawr at Dolbenmaen, and it is clear that by the twelfth century, when the Norman fashion of building earthen mounds (or mottes) for castles of wood was being copied by the Welsh, the residence or *llys* of the lord of the commote or at least one of his strongholds was at the mound still existing in that village. It is admirably situated to command the route at a river crossing just where high ground, suitable for ambuscade, approaches it on both sides. It is probable that this castle-mound remained in use until the foundation of Criccieth Castle.

So far as is known, before the early thirteenth century the only buildings at or near the site of the present castle and town of Criccieth were the church and any concomitant buildings in its immediate vicinity. Save that there may have been a prehistoric camp on the castle rock, there is no evidence that any earlier fortification preceded the existing structure.

The first reference to a castle at Criccieth occurs in 1239, when it is recorded that Dafydd, son of Llywelyn ap Iorwerth, "seized his brother, Gruffydd, breaking the compact with him,

The published report of B.H. St J. O'Neil's work at the castle (By kind permission of the Cambrian Archaeological Association).

Medieval key, probably of thirteenth-century date, found during excavations at the castle (By permission of the National Museum of Wales).

Sculptured capital, of thirteenth-century date, found during excavations at the castle.

Llywelyn ab Iorwerth: First Welsh Castle

THE EARLIEST PART of the castle consists of the inner ward built on the highest point of the hill by Llywelyn ab Iorwerth (Llywelyn the Great), probably sometime between 1230 and his death in 1240. The natural sea-cliff defences were supplemented by the construction of earthwork defences on the more vulnerable landward side.

The faced masonry of this period is characterized by the use of angular naturally-split stones, quarried from the castle rock or from Dinas, a small hillock immediately to the west of the castle, interspersed with large beach or glacial boulders. The mortar which held this masonry together was made of beach gravel and was rather sandy and grey in appearance.

The principal structure took the form of an impressive gatehouse comprising two 'D'-shaped towers, set side by side. Elongated 'D'-shaped or apsidal towers of this type were being built, principally as keeps, by the rulers of Gwynedd during the first half of the thirteenth century, and examples have survived at sites as far apart as Ewloe in the north-eastern corner of Wales, Carndochan above Bala, and Castell y Bere north of Tywyn (Meirionnydd).

By the end of the second decade of the thirteenth century Llywelyn had become the premier native lord in Wales, a position reflected in the marriage alliances he contracted with leading English lords of the Welsh March. Notable amongst these were the marriages of his daughters Gwladus, to Reginald de Braose, and Helen to John the Scot, the nephew and heir of Ranulf de Blundeville, the earl of Chester.

A reconstruction showing Ranulph de Blundeville's inner gatehouse at Beeston Castle, with a later stone ramp leading up to the entrance (Illustration by Ivan Lapper, by kind permission of English Heritage).

Upon his return from the Crusades in 1220, Ranulf de Blundeville had embarked upon a major programme of castle-building. The inner gatehouse of his new castle at Beeston, just over the English border in Cheshire, bears such a marked similarity to the inner gatehouse at Criccieth that it may be suggested that, ten to fifteen years later, Llywelyn may well have modelled his design on that of his ally.

An aerial view of Castell y Bere from the south-west.

It is also of interest to note that in 1228, and again in 1231, Llywelyn attacked the new castle that was being built at Montgomery by his enemy, Hubert de Burgh. That castle, eventually completed in 1232, has a strong gatehouse with an irregularly-shaped inner ward strikingly similar in design to that at Criccieth. Llywelyn's construction of a gatehouse of an advanced type at Criccieth would seem to be quite consistent with his standing as the pre-eminent Welsh lord, and the ally or formidable opponent of the Marcher lords. Indeed, the gatehouse may well have been constructed with the assistance of English masons.

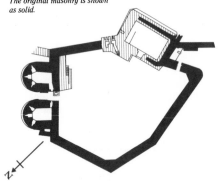

Sketch plans of Llywelyn ab Iorwerth's inner ward at Criccieth Castle (left), and Hubert de Burgh's inner ward at Montgomery Castle (right). The original masonry is shown as solid.

A reconstruction of the castle as it might have appeared in about 1240 (Illustration by Ivan Lapper).

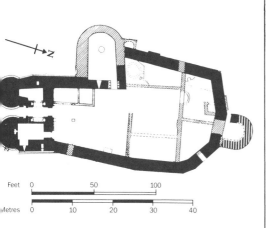

Feet | 0 | 50 | 100

Metres | 0 | 10 | 20 | 30 | 40

Above: *A stone head, possibly of Llywelyn ab Iorwerth, found at Deganwy Castle (By permission of the National Museum of Wales).*

Below: *Hubert de Burgh was one of the leading protagonists in the English attempt to contain the power of Llywelyn the Great. Henry III granted him Montgomery Castle in 1228. This manuscript illustration by Matthew Paris shows him taking sanctuary at Merton Priory on his final fall from power (By permission of the British Library, Royal Ms. 14 C VII, f.119).*

Llywelyn ap Gruffudd: The Welsh Castle Enlarged

BETWEEN 1255, when he became the sole ruler of Gwynedd, and his death in 1282, Llywelyn ap Gruffudd (Llywelyn the Last) enlarged the castle by adding the outer ward. The most likely date for this work would be sometime during the 1260s or early 1270s. The remaining area of the hilltop, to the north and south of the first castle, was enclosed by a curtain wall, and new towers were constructed at the northern and south-western corners.

The coat of arms of Llywelyn ap Gruffudd.

The outer gate, at the southern corner, now became the principal entrance to the castle. All this work was characterized by the use of a

Sculptured capital, of thirteenth century date, showing traces of a female head, found during excavation at the castle (By permission of the National Museum of Wales).

different style of masonry with a different mortar from that of the first period. The face of the masonry, which is not regularly coursed, is composed of large split boulders and large hewn stones, derived not from the castle rock, but from elsewhere, and includes slates which in places give the walls a bluish-grey tint. The mortar was more gravelly than that of the first phase.

The only alterations within the inner ward consisted of widening the external stair leading up to the first-floor entrance, at the rear of the gatehouse, and the insertion of a ground-floor entrance into the south-east tower.

King Edward I: English Rebuilding

NO DETAILS SURVIVE of the capture of the castle by Edward I's forces, although we know that it was in English hands by 14 March 1283. During the period 1283-92 in the region of £500 may have been spent on works at the site. That this was a substantial sum for the time may be judged by the outlay of only half that sum in building the two western towers of the inner ward at nearby Harlech Castle (each four storeys high with a battlemented turret). What, therefore, was all this money spent on at Criccieth?

The contemporary building accounts, whilst itemizing expenditure, provide few clues as to which structures it was actually spent upon. We are therefore, once again, dependent upon the evidence of the surviving masonry, where

The reverse of the great seal of King Edward I (By permission of the British Library).

The two western towers of the inner ward at Harlech.

a third period can be clearly identified. The masonry is composed almost entirely of stone quarried from the castle rock, or nearby Dinas, and in places the stones appear to have been roughly-squared and laid in almost regular courses. The mortar resembled that used in the previous period but contained more and larger shells.

This masonry can be identified in: *(i)* the first raising of the inner gatehouse to the level of the embrasures, which were blocked up in the final phase; *(ii)* the final addition to the stair against the rear of the gatehouse; *(iii)* the rebuilding and refacing of the south-east tower and the addition of masonry, leading to latrines, against its courtyard-facing side; *(iv)* the stonework of the south-west tower above about 7 feet (2.1m) from the ground, and the addition of an external stair leading to its first floor; and *(v)* the extension of the outer gatehouse.

The picture that emerges from all this work is one of a very major rebuilding of the castle, with the south-west and south-east towers being substantially reconstructed from the ground floor upwards. Because of the ruinous nature of much of the surviving masonry, we cannot now determine how much rebuilding work was also necessary to the outer curtain wall or to the northern tower.

Generally, Welsh towers appear to have consisted of a ground floor or basement with the main apartment on the floor above. It is very unusual for them to have stood above two storeys high. It seems unlikely, therefore, that, as originally constructed, any of the rectangular towers at Criccieth stood above this height. All three may have been substantially damaged during the capture of the castle by Edward I's forces. At the same time as repairing them, the south-west and south-east towers could well have been raised by an extra floor. Indeed, the latrine shafts in the refaced masonry at opposite corners of the south-east tower may have served latrines at both first- and second-floor levels.

It seems unlikely that the north tower would have served as an engine tower during the Welsh period, and this may have been remodelled for this purpose, with the addition of a wide shallow external stair, during this later period.

Other works which would have been included within the expenditure at this time were the provision of new buildings within the castle, such as the King's Hall, mentioned in 1296, and the probable remodelling and recutting of the earthwork defences on the north-west side.

Aerial view of Criccieth Castle from the north-west.

King Edward II: Further Repairs

A S WE HAVE SEEN, over £250 was spent on works at the castle between 1307 and 1327. Again, such a sum should represent a fairly significant amount of work. References to the raising of the wall of the 'twin' and Cistern towers suggests that the upper part of the gatehouse was rebuilt and, indeed, this work can be seen in the surviving masonry where the embrasures of Edward I's gatehouse have been blocked up and the whole structure raised. This may have been occasioned by the

A reconstruction of the castle as it might have appeared at the beginning of the fourteenth century (Illustration by Ivan Lapper).

need to repair and reroof the gatehouse, together with a desire to gain extra height and improve the view out over the north tower.

A certain amount of work was also undertaken on the Mountfort and Leyburn towers, probably involving repairs to their roofs and upper masonry. Although neither tower can be identified with certainty, it seems likely that they were either the south-east or south-west towers, both of which are now too ruined for any structural evidence of this work to survive. The King's Hall and various other internal buildings were also under repair and this all seems to have been part of a general refurbishment to buildings throughout the castle, necessitated by decay in the years that followed Edward I's rebuilding.

Tour of the Castle

T HE FOLLOWING TOUR guides the visitor around the castle by what it is hoped
will be an interesting and, in starting with the earliest part of the structure,
logical way. By dividing it into individual sections, each dealing with a different
part of the castle, the tour will also cater for those visitors who prefer to find their
own way around, perhaps just consulting the text here and there.

The Approach and Outer Defences

T HE LOWER PART of the path leading up
the hill from the entrance follows the
approximate line of the late thirteenth-
century approach to the castle. Where the
modern path turns to the right, its medieval
predecessor carried straight on around the
northern and eastern sides of the castle to the
outer gatehouse. This line of approach was
largely destroyed by later quarrying on the
cliff face.

Continuing up the path, pause when you
are just below the western tower of the
gatehouse. Immediately to your left is the
well-laid masonry of the ruined north tower.
Extending to the right of this tower, between
you and the gatehouse, is a low wall
representing all that remains of the outer

*Inset left: Modern entrance to the outer ward of the castle with one of
the splays of the original arrowslit showing on the left.*

*Inset right: The lower part of the latrine, with an arched outlet, on the
western side of the inner gatehouse.*

18

curtain wall on this side of the castle. Turning about and looking downhill you can see the two lines of earthwork defences which stretched from cliff to cliff on the western side of the castle rock. The upper bank is immediately in front of you. Outside there is a ditch. The slight traces of an outer bank can be detected just behind the custodian's office.

At the top of the path visitors enter the castle through a breach in the outer curtain wall at a point where there was once an arrowslit, one side of which can clearly be seen in the splayed masonry on the right. In order to see the castle in the same sequence as that in which it was built, you should now turn immediately to the left and walk up the passage (path) between the inner and outer curtain walls towards the front of the inner gatehouse. Notice near the end of the passage, on the right, that there is a rectangular projection, with an arched outlet, in the angle between the west gatehouse tower and the inner curtain wall. This housed latrines at first-and second-floor levels in the gatehouse. Before the construction of the outer curtain wall these probably discharged down the face of the castle rock. Continue around to the front of the gatehouse and stand back beside the stairs leading up to the north (Engine) tower. From here you have a good view of the front of both gatehouse towers and the entrance passage leading between them into the inner ward (the north tower itself will be described at the end of the tour).

An aerial view of the castle from the east.

Inner Ward

THE INNER WARD, situated on the highest point of the castle rock, consists of the great gatehouse, the south-east tower and an encircling curtain wall, against the inner face of which would have been constructed such buildings as the hall and kitchen. The original external rendering still survives in places on the walls.

Inner Gatehouse

THE GATEHOUSE consists of two towers of D-shaped plan flanking the entrance passage. Three building phases can be clearly seen on the outer face of each of these towers. The first phase consists of all the masonry up to a point just above a line of square holes about 8 feet (2.5m) below the top of the walls. This

The inner gatehouse from the north, showing the change of build, with blocked up battlements, above the line of square holes and near the top of both towers.

walling is characterized by the use of a mixture of angular, naturally-split stones quarried from the rock on which the castle is built, interspersed with large beach or glacial boulders, and must date to the initial building period of Llywelyn ab Iorwerth. At ground level, the gatehouse was defended by three arrowslits in each of the towers. Also belonging to this period is the above-mentioned latrine projection on the outer face of the west gatehouse tower.

In the second phase, probably dating to the time of Edward I, the battlements appear to have been rebuilt, using better-laid angular blocks of the castle rock. The large square holes below the battlements held horizontal beams for a temporary or permanent timber *hourd*, or fighting platform, which projected out from the wallface. The final phase, which probably belongs to the second decade of the fourteenth century, witnessed the blocking up of the second-phase battlements and a further raising of the gatehouse walls to their present level. One of the arrowslits from this period survives at the top of the eastern gatehouse tower.

The entrance passage, with the bottom of a portcullis groove on the left.

entrance was protected by a portcullis. The grooves which held this in place can be seen in the masonry on either side of the passage. About 7 feet (2.1m) further along the passage the side walls are rebated to take a pair of doors, and the butt of one of the iron crooks upon which they were hung can be seen embedded in the masonry, low down behind the right-hand door rebate. Doors beyond, on either side of the passage, lead into the ground-floor guardrooms.

A timber floor originally extended right across the gatehouse at first-floor level, probably arranged so that some of the floor boards over the entrance passageway could be removed in order to drop missiles on unwelcome intruders.

At the inner end of the entrance passage a modern iron grille covers a water cistern, fed by

The upper part of the western gatehouse tower, showing two changes of build and blocked up battlements.

The arch at the front of the gatehouse passage is a modern rebuild inserted before the castle came into State care. The paved surface of the entrance passage is also modern. As you pass along the passageway, you will see that, in addition to the arrowslits in the ground-floor guardchambers, the

Water cistern beneath modern grille in the gate-passage.

a natural spring, which provided the castle garrison with fresh water. This originally had a wooden cover and its rather inconvenient location may have been occasioned by the discovery of a spring in that position during the castle's construction.

The gatehouse is too ruinous for it to be possible to provide public access to the upper rooms and these are best viewed from the ground-floor guardchambers. As has already been mentioned, each guardchamber was provided with three arrowslits facing out into

Arrowslits on the inside of the western gatehouse tower.

the field. Archaeological excavation within these rooms revealed a distinct layer of burning overlying the floors and this was probably associated with the capture and subsequent destruction of the castle by Owain Glyndŵr.

A fine crucifix was found in this layer in the western (right) guardchamber, suggesting that one of the upper rooms might have served as the castle chapel.

A gilded copper-alloy crucifix figure found during excavations in the western tower of the gatehouse (By permission of the National Museum of Wales).

The upper two storeys were divided up into separate rooms by timber partitions and all the rooms within the gatehouse had plastered walls. Doorways in the western tower lead to latrines at both first- and second-floor levels. In keeping with the defensive nature of the

Upper storeys in the eastern tower of the gatehouse.

gatehouse, there are no forward-facing windows at any level, and the only surviving window on the upper floors is at first-floor level on the naturally well defended east side. The upper rooms in the gatehouse were probably lit by windows in the least vulnerable, but now missing, inward-facing rear wall. This wall may have also contained fireplaces to warm these rooms and during the excavation of debris in the entrance passageway parts of a chimney were found.

Leaving the passage and turning to the left, at the rear of the eastern tower of the gatehouse you will see the remains of three

The stairway at the back of the gatehouse leading up to the first-floor doorway.

separate phases of a stairway which originally provided access to the first-floor rooms of the gatehouse. All that remains of the first stair, consisting of the mortared beds of three steps, can be seen above and behind the second-phase stairway leading to the threshold of the first-floor doorway, part of the right-hand jamb of which still survives. This stair probably dates to the first gatehouse of Llywelyn ab Iorwerth. In the next phase, probably dating to the time of Llywelyn ap Gruffudd, the stairway was widened. Finally, as part of the alterations undertaken by Edward I, the south wall of the first stairway was raised and extended to the curtain wall and the area between this and the gatehouse was filled in. At the same time the second-phase stairway was widened on its south side. Whilst this widened stairway provided access to the first-floor doorway, a new wooden stair extended up over the infilled first-phase stair to the inner ward curtain wall. From here a doorway led into the second floor of the gatehouse and a straight stair extended up in the thickness of the wall to the gatehouse wall-walk.

South-East Tower

LEAVING THE GATEHOUSE, follow the south curtain wall on the seaward side of the castle, to the remains of the south-east tower. This has been very extensively altered since it was first built by Llywelyn ab Iorwerth. By looking at the guidebook plan, you will see how the early masonry has been encased in later work. If you leave the inner ward by the small postern gate in the south-eastern (far) corner

The interior of the south-east tower looking east.

and examine the exterior of the tower, you can observe the evidence for this. On your left, just through the doorway, you can see that the main curtain wall extends into the body of the masonry of the tower. The same thing can be seen on the exterior of the opposite (north-eastern) side of the tower in the area of masonry between the base of a latrine chute on the north face of the tower

Above: *The base of a single latrine-chute on the north face of the south-east tower, and four similar chutes on the adjoining stretch of curtain wall.*

The base of a latrine-chute at the southern corner of the south-east tower.

and the four latrine chutes on the adjoining section of curtain wall. This structural evidence suggests that the original tower has been completely refaced. Return to the inner ward and to the entrance to the south-east tower, noting as you do, the base of a further latrine chute in the southern corner of the tower.

Originally, there must have been a step up from the courtyard to the ground-floor entrance of the south-east tower. Enough evidence survives to demonstrate that there were two-leafed doors at both the outer and inner ends of the entrance. The bottom stones of the outer door jambs still survive, each with a groove that originally held the lowermost of the two iron crooks upon which the doors were hung.

A Bird's-Eye View of Criccieth Castle from the North-East

with notes on some of the principal features

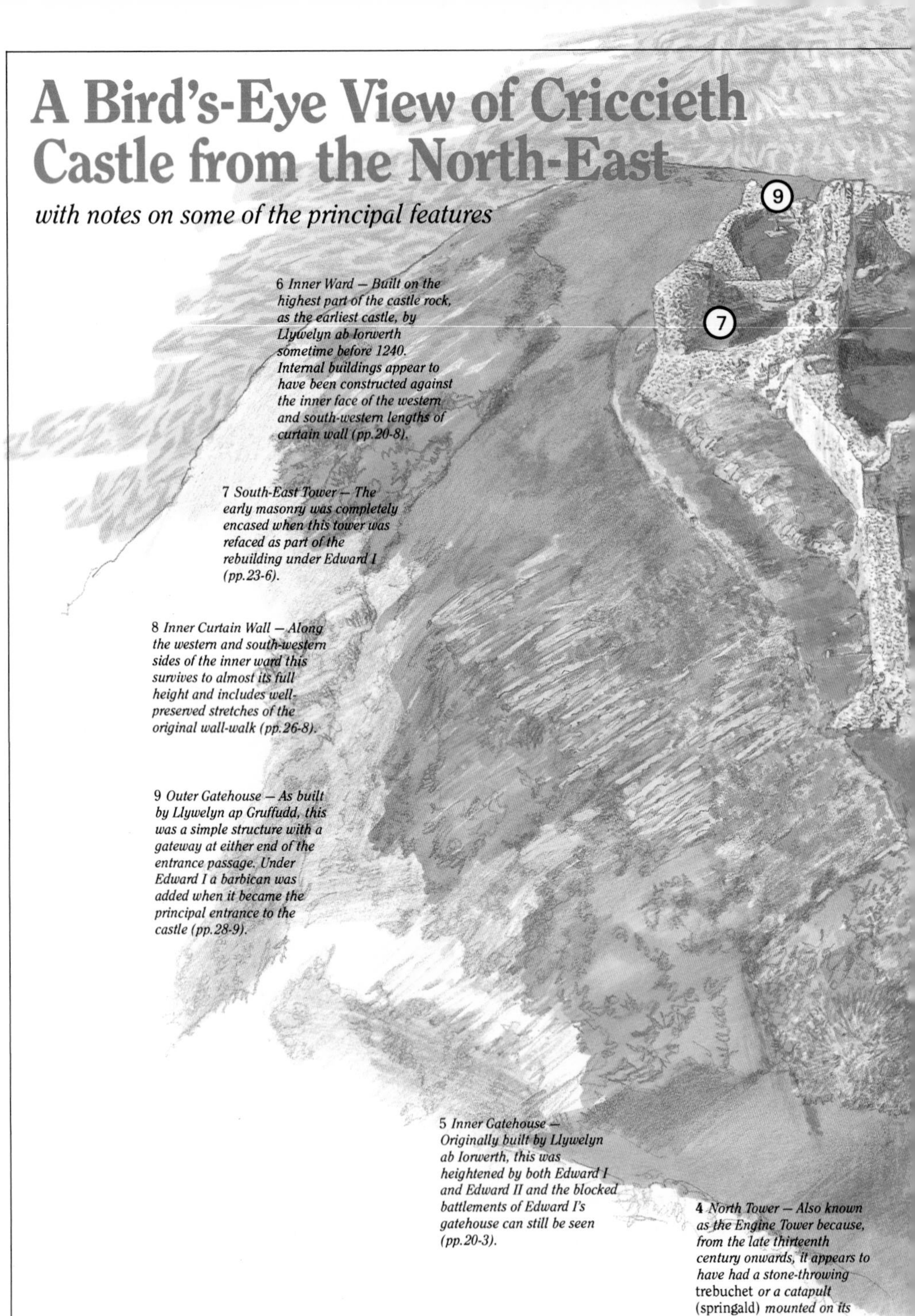

9

7

6 *Inner Ward — Built on the highest part of the castle rock, as the earliest castle, by Llywelyn ab Iorwerth sometime before 1240. Internal buildings appear to have been constructed against the inner face of the western and south-western lengths of curtain wall (pp.20-8).*

7 *South-East Tower — The early masonry was completely encased when this tower was refaced as part of the rebuilding under Edward I (pp.23-6).*

8 *Inner Curtain Wall — Along the western and south-western sides of the inner ward this survives to almost its full height and includes well-preserved stretches of the original wall-walk (pp.26-8).*

9 *Outer Gatehouse — As built by Llywelyn ap Gruffudd, this was a simple structure with a gateway at either end of the entrance passage. Under Edward I a barbican was added when it became the principal entrance to the castle (pp.28-9).*

5 *Inner Gatehouse — Originally built by Llywelyn ab Iorwerth, this was heightened by both Edward I and Edward II and the blocked battlements of Edward I's gatehouse can still be seen (pp.20-3).*

4 *North Tower — Also known as the Engine Tower because, from the late thirteenth century onwards, it appears to have had a stone-throwing trebuchet or a catapult (springald) mounted on its roof (p.31).*

24

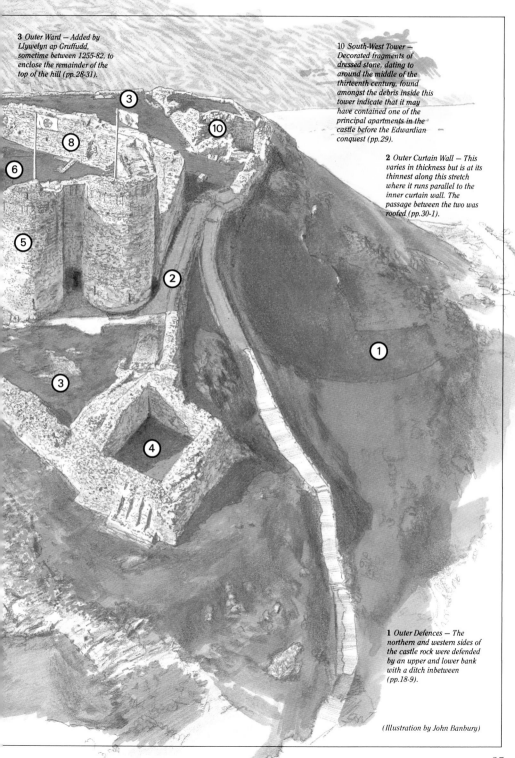

3 *Outer Ward — Added by Llywelyn ap Gruffudd, sometime between 1255-82, to enclose the remainder of the top of the hill (pp.28-31).*

10 *South-West Tower — Decorated fragments of dressed stone, dating to around the middle of the thirteenth century, found amongst the debris inside this tower indicate that it may have contained one of the principal apartments in the castle before the Edwardian conquest (pp.29).*

2 *Outer Curtain Wall — This varies in thickness but is at its thinnest along this stretch where it runs parallel to the inner curtain wall. The passage between the two was roofed (pp.30-1).*

1 *Outer Defences — The northern and western sides of the castle rock were defended by an upper and lower bank with a ditch inbetween (pp.18-9).*

(Illustration by John Banbury)

The long slot which held the timber draw-bar to secure the door can be seen in the masonry on the right. The remains of two further door crooks can be seen embedded in the left-hand jamb of the inner door. It became clear during the consolidation of this

The inner door jamb on the left-hand side of the doorway to the south-east tower, with the stump of one of the iron door crooks still surviving between the lowermost stone and the one above it.

doorway that it was a later insertion, probably dating to the time of Llywelyn ap Gruffudd, and that the initial access to this level must have been down a wooden stair from the floor above.

When excavated the interior of this tower had the same burnt destruction level overlying its floor as that found in the gatehouse. The burning was so intense that in places it had redenned the masonry of the walls. The original floor level was slightly higher than the present surface and covered much of the bedrock. The platform of masonry on the left was the base of a stone stair leading up to the first floor. This was later dismantled, with access to the upper level being provided from the curtain wall, or possibly by a stone stair against the inner face of the curtain wall and over the entrance to the latrines just to the north of the tower.

Only the masonry in the south-west corner survives to any height and here, at first-floor level, one side and part of the back of a fireplace can be seen. Chimney fragments were found in the destruction debris immediately below this fireplace. The fact that there are two latrine chutes in the outer face on opposite sides of this tower may be evidence that it once extended up a further floor, with a latrine at either level.

Two stone chimneys reconstructed from pieces found in the south-west corner of the south-east tower, the inner gatehouse and the south-west tower. The chimneys are probably of late thirteenth or early fourteenth century date.

Inner Curtain Wall and Internal Buildings

IMMEDIATELY TO THE RIGHT of the south-east tower, as you leave by the doorway, is a large block of masonry built against the original inner face of the curtain wall. This contained two stairs which led up from the

Two stairways against the inner face of the curtain wall to the north of the south-east tower.

courtyard to two pairs of latrines. The stair nearest to the south-east tower is complete. That further north, which originally rose against the face of the wall, is now ruined. It is possible that as well as leading to one of the latrines, this stair may also have continued upwards, over the passage to the other latrine, and on up to the first floor of the south-east tower.

With the exception of the length between the gatehouse and the south-east tower, the curtain wall of the inner ward survives to almost its full height, retaining well-preserved stretches of the original wall-walk. The masonry at the southern and western corners of the inner ward has been deliberately thickened to strengthen and make more defensible these awkward, pointed, angles.

The original parapet, with one side of an embrasure, can still be seen standing to its full height of nearly 8 feet (2.5m) where it joins the rear of the western gate tower. The remains of small arrowslits are also visible at parapet level along the western and south-western sides of the inner ward, and these

Below: An arrowslit at parapet level in the western curtain wall of the inner ward.

Bottom: The western side of the inner ward, with the gatehouse to the right.

appear to have alternated with embrasures throughout the entire length of the battlements. Also on the western and south-western sides there are channels through the wall, below wall-walk level, for the discharge of rainwater outside the curtain. This suggests that internal buildings were probably constructed against the inner ward curtain wall, with these drains carrying rainwater away from their roofs.

Although no evidence of any of the internal buildings was found during archaeological excavations, this may merely reflect the form of their construction, particularly if they were of timber, rather than their absence altogether. Indeed, the King's Hall, mentioned in 1296, may well have been constructed against the straight stretch of curtain wall behind the gatehouse, on the north-western side, and beam-holes in the other two straight stretches of curtain on the western and south-western sides must indicate the position of other buildings.

It will be noted that sections of facing-stone are missing at several points on the inside of the inner curtain wall. This is where modern repairs, undertaken before the castle came into State care, were removed during consolidation work to reveal the medieval masonry.

The wall footings near the southern gate of the inner ward were excavated when the masonry of the castle was being consolidated.

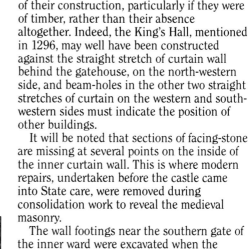

It was not possible at that time to determine their function, but the circular area may be

A possible oven base near the south gate.

the base of an oven, or associated with metal working. The fact that these structures would have obstructed the entrance suggests that they may post-date its main use.

South Gate

IN THE FIRST PERIOD, during the time of Llywelyn ab Iorwerth, this entrance acted as a simple footgate or postern. It later provided a means of access between the inner and outer wards at this end of the castle. The two large slots on either side of the passage originally held the vertical timbers of a very substantial door frame. On the left are the holes for the draw-bars to secure the door when closed. You should now pass through this door into the outer ward which will be described next.

The south gate with the excavated footings of later structures in the foreground.

Outer Ward

DURING THE SECOND PERIOD of the castle's history, when it was held by Llywelyn ab Iorwerth's grandson, Llywelyn ap Gruffudd, the remaining area of the hilltop was enclosed by a curtain wall. A new gateway was provided at the southern corner; a spacious new tower with ornate decoration was constructed in the south-western corner; and a substantial tower, built of well-laid masonry, occupied the northern end, in front of the earlier gatehouse.

We shall examine the structures in the outer ward in a clockwise direction, starting with the stone platform immediately outside the south gate of the inner ward. The clue to the function of this structure is provided by a stone channel, which once contained a lead pipe, suggesting that it formed the base for a cistern or water tank.

The outer curtain wall butts up against the outer face of the south-east tower. Just

Stone channel for a lead waterpipe.

beyond the platform it widens for a short stretch perhaps to accommodate a stair leading up onto the wall-walk. The narrow wall then continues to the outer gatehouse into which it is bonded.

Outer Gatehouse

THE ORIGINAL OUTER GATEHOUSE was a simple structure, consisting of a passage leading through the curtain wall to a gateway at the inner end. A second gate was later added at the outer end of the passage. Later still, probably during the time of Edward I, the gateway was extended outwards by the addition of two new side walls which provided extra protection in the form of a simple barbican. A short length of wall can be seen just inside the outer ward against the eastern (left-hand) face of the eastern wall of the

The outer gatehouse from within the outer ward looking east.

gatehouse. It has been suggested that this may have been part of a wall which extended across this section of the outer ward to the southern corner of the inner ward. This barrier would have prevented direct, uncontrolled, access from the outer gate to the inner ward.

The narrow curtain wall continues along the south side of the castle rock to the south-west tower. Unfortunately, the wall is too ruinous at the junction between the two to establish their original structural relationship.

South-West Tower

THIS IS LOCATED near the path by which you entered the castle. As built by Llywelyn ap Gruffudd, it would probably have consisted of a basement with one upper storey and been similar to the original rectangular tower, built

The interior of the south-west tower looking north.

by Llywelyn ab Iorwerth at Dolwyddelan, in the heart of Snowdonia.

In the first phase, the ground floor or basement of the tower would have been reached by a ladder or wooden stair from the floor above. The purpose of the stone foundation in the northern corner of the room is unknown, but it possibly formed the base for this wooden stair. A ground-floor entrance was inserted as part of Edward I's rebuilding of the tower towards the end of the thirteenth century. Two narrow lights or slits in large embrasures flanked the doorway. Isolated flat stones within the room are all that remains of the surface upon which a wooden floor was probably laid.

If you look at the inner face of the highest section of wall, at the northern end of the tower, you will be able to see two distinct building periods in the masonry. The earliest work consists of the lower 7 feet (2.1m) made up predominantly of roughly-laid boulders and quarried stone brought in from elsewhere. Above this, the wall is composed almost exclusively of orange-coloured medium and large stones, which are roughly-coursed and quarried from the castle rock. Both this masonry and that of the lower part of the wall has been burnt red, like the walls of the south-east tower, no doubt during Glyndŵr's destruction.

As you leave the tower, notice the decorated door-stop on the right-hand side of the outer door, and a stone-lined drain against the outer face of the wall. Turning to your left, you will find similar door-stops at the bottom of a stone stairway built against the outer, north, face of this tower. This stairway is constructed of the same masonry as that of the upper walls of the tower and, like the secondary ground-floor doorway to the tower, must date to Edward I's rebuilding of the castle.

Fragments of dressed and decorated stone, dating to around the middle of the thirteenth century, were found amongst the debris on the floor inside this tower, suggesting that it might have housed one of the principal apartments in the castle before the Edwardian conquest. The tower must have been substantially rebuilt, refaced and probably raised by an extra storey as part of Edward I's reconstruction of the castle.

Outer Curtain Wall

THE CURTAIN WALL of the outer ward extends northwards from the south-west tower, along the western edge of the castle rock, to the north tower. The first part of this line is bonded into the corner of the south-west tower, beyond which it extends north as a thick wall until it is adjacent with the western corner of the inner ward. This stretch includes three arrowslits with wide embrasures. That next to the south-west tower must have been blocked up when the external stair to the first floor was added. The third embrasure along has been breached and now forms the modern entrance to the castle (see p.19).

Below: *The outer face of the north-western curtain wall of the inner ward, with the lower two lines of holes indicating the position of a pent roof over the passage between the inner and outer curtain walls.*

Bottom: *The outer curtain wall looking northwards along the western edge of the castle.*

You should now retrace the route you took when you first entered the castle, but this time we shall be concentrating on the outer curtain wall and the north tower. The outer curtain wall, on your left, is now much narrower only widening again when it has run north beyond the masonry of the inner ward.

Nowhere is there a clearer demonstration that the inner ward comprises the earliest castle. The outer curtain is narrow because it has to be squeezed onto the edge of the castle rock, leaving sufficient room for a passage between it and the west curtain wall of the inner ward. In fact, this narrow passage was originally roofed and the lower two lines of holes on the outer face of the west curtain wall of the inner ward, on the latrine projection and on the west face of the gatehouse, would have held the rafters and joists of a pent roof. The uppermost line of holes on the outer face of the inner curtain wall are for the roof drain-outlets mentioned previously.

Two V-shaped arrowslits can be seen at the southern end of the thin outer curtain wall and there may have been others along this stretch which have not survived. There is another arrowslit with a wide embrasure just to the south of the north tower where the curtain wall has resumed its full width. This wider wall only partially bonds into the south-west side of the north tower.

The remaining length of outer curtain wall extends from the north tower, along the eastern edge of the castle rock, to the north-eastern corner of the inner ward, against which it is straight-jointed. If you look just to the right of the north tower you will see a blocked arrowslit of the wide embrasure type, and here the arch over the embrasure has survived. Both stretches of wider wall would have carried a wall-walk with battlements.

North Tower

THIS TOWER is also known as the Engine tower as it appears to have had an engine, such as a stone-throwing *trebuchet* or a catapult (*springald*), mounted on its roof. The

The north tower viewed from the inner gatehouse to the south.

tower is well-built, with an outer face of quarried or hewn stones which are a bluish-grey in colour. The walls have a pronounced batter on the three sides which face the field on the slope of the hill and, by projecting forward from the line of the adjoining curtain walls, they afford a good field of fire.

On the lower face of the north-eastern (outer) side of the tower there are two pairs of latrines which must have served the first floor and battlements. The sockets for the floor joists of the first floor can be seen in the top of the surviving masonry of the wall next to

the staircase. The basement of the tower was unlit and can have only been accessible by a wooden ladder from the floor above. Presumably it was used for storage.

The external stone staircase on the south-eastern side of the tower was probably added as part of Edward I's work. The fact that it was well-built and gently sloping suggests that, in addition to providing access to the first floor, it might have been a means of helping to raise ammunition to the engine on the roof.

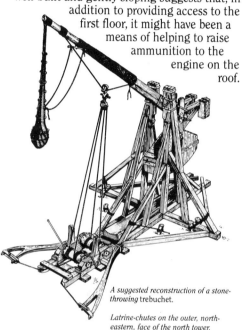

A suggested reconstruction of a stone-throwing trebuchet.

Latrine-chutes on the outer, north-eastern, face of the north tower.

It is hoped that this tour will have provided the visitor with a fairly full picture of the structural history of the castle as we understand it at present. However, it cannot be over-emphasized that the very ruinous nature of much of the castle will always leave questions about its history and building sequence unanswered.

Pennarth Fawr
Medieval Hall-House

Introduction

AT FIRST SIGHT the late-medieval
hall-house at Pennarth Fawr, with
its plain stone exterior and later
windows, is an unprepossessing building.
However, the moment of discovery comes
when you walk through the door to be
faced with a superb carved timber interior
which was faithfully restored in the late
1930s.

Pennarth Fawr is a fine example of the type
of dwelling occupied by the Welsh upper
classes or gentry from the fourteenth century
to the middle of the sixteenth century.
Houses with this type of simple rectangular
plan were usually divided into three parts
consisting of a central hall, open to the roof,
with separate suites of rooms at either end. At
one end of the hall was the cross passage with
doors at either end; at the other was the
raised dais upon which the high table stood.
Here, the lord and his guests ate at the table.
A canopy, often elaborately carved, protected
them from soot and smuts produced by the
fire which took the form of an open hearth in
the centre of the room with smoke escaping
through a louvre in the roof.

The windows, at least initially, could be
closed only with shutters. Ventilation and
light were provided by keeping the windows
on the windward side shuttered and opening
those on the leeward side; the shutters could,

Ground Plan of the House

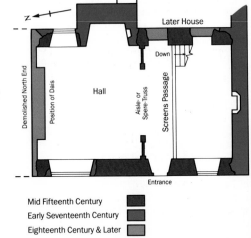

Mid Fifteenth Century

Early Seventeenth Century

Eighteenth Century & Later

in this way, be adjusted according to wind
direction.

Partitions beyond the passage and behind
the dais separated the service rooms and
apartments from the hall and divided the
building into three units. The two end units
were rarely equal in size and their layout
varied from building to building. In some
cases a single large parlour or a smaller
parlour with a service room occupied the dais
end with the main service rooms being
located beyond the passage; in others the
service rooms, consisting of the buttery and
pantry, were behind the dais with a parlour or
occasionally an animal byre at the passage
end. Both ends of the building were usually
two-storeyed.

The main distribution of surviving hall-
houses within Wales is in the north-east and
English border areas where they are usually of
half-timbered construction. Pennarth Fawr, in
the true tradition of north-west Wales, has
load-bearing stone walls.

General view of the house from the west.

History

P ENNARTH FAWR was probably built around the middle of the fifteenth century by Madog ap Howel ap Madog, a descendant of Einion ap Gruffudd. The house was located in the southernmost part of the township of Pennarth. It was associated with a relatively small parcel of land of 97 acres (39.2ha) but formed the principal residence for its owners, who also had other landholdings in the area, until well into the eighteenth century.

Pennarth Fawr was inherited by Madog's son, Howel ap Madog, and then by his son, William ap Howel who died in about 1540. William's son, John, adopted the surname Gwyn or Wynn and he married Jonet by whom he had four sons and three daughters. The eldest son, Hugh Gwyn, was High Sheriff of Caernarvonshire in 1599-1600 and it was he who modernized the house by replacing the open fire, which stood in the middle of the hall, with the large fireplace in the east, lateral wall. His shield of arms, bearing the date [16]15, can be seen above the fireplace.

The building underwent further alterations at the hands of Hugh Gwyn's grandson, John Wynn, who inserted a first floor in the hall.

Hugh Gwyn's shield of arms over the fireplace, bearing the date [16]15.

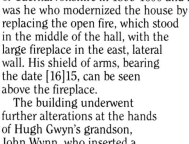

A reconstruction of how the interior of the house may have appeared in the late fifteenth century (Illustration by Dylan Roberts).

This is commemorated on a beam, which can still be seen amongst the dismantled timbers in the hall, inscribed W/II 1656 FEB 20. John Wynn was still living in 1662 when he was

A beam inscribed W/II 1656 FEB 20 commemorating John Wynn's insertion of a first floor in the hall.

taxed for three hearths at Pennarth Fawr in the Hearth Tax Assessment of that year.

The house passed down through the female line until in 1886 the lands in Pennarth were sold for £8,550 to Owen Evans of Broom Hall. In 1937 William Evans of Broom Hall undertook a major programme of work on the house to return it to its original medieval state. Over the years it had been completely altered and modernized into what appeared to be a normal farmhouse with an upper floor and various separate rooms, so that hardly anything of the present spacious interior was visible. The restored house came into State care in 1949 and is now maintained by Cadw: Welsh Historic Monuments, on behalf of the Secretary of State for Wales.

Description

Exterior

VISITORS SHOULD start by looking at the outside of the building from the garden. The house is built of roughly-coursed local rubble with a foundation of large rounded boulders. The plain slate roof, which is modern, has a chimney stack at either end although that at the northern end (to the left) no longer serves any surviving fireplaces. Part of the far, eastern, side of the building is masked by a wing which was added in the seventeenth century. The present south wall (to the right) and the cellar were also built at that time. The north wall, built of better laid masonry than the rest of the house, was added in the eighteenth century and may have replaced an earlier timber partition at that end of the building. This partition and the later wall would have originally separated the hall from

the apartments to the north of it, which appear to have been demolished sometime during the nineteenth century.

All the window-frames in the building are modern and only one window, that to the south of the present entrance, is in its original position. The large window opening to the north of the door is almost certainly an enlargement of the original main window of the hall, which would have lit the dais end.

Screens Passage and Service Rooms

UPON ENTERING the house you will find yourself in the screens passage which extends across the width of the building separating the hall from the service rooms. The blocked door at its opposite end once led out into a yard and probably to the kitchen. On the right of the passage the regularly spaced mortise

The main first-floor beam on the south side of the screens passage, with holes for the wooden pegs to secure the upper ends of the timbers of a panel and post screen.

holes cut into the upper side of a timber beam set into the floor mark the position of the vertical timbers of a panel-and-post screen. The upper ends of these timbers were secured with round wooden pegs into mortises set into a groove on the underside of the main first-floor beam. Above, small round holes in the surviving original timbers of the roof truss show that this partition was carried up to the apex of the roof in wattle and daub.

There is no distinctive break in the spacing of the mortises in the ground-floor beam (except near the far end where a piece of timber has been replaced), and it is difficult to be certain of the position of the doorways in the screen between the passage and the rooms to the right. A modern ladder-type stair at what would have been the western end of the screen leads up to the first floor. The exact design and position of the original stair is unknown. The character of this end of the building was substantially altered in the nineteenth century when the east-facing windows, at both ground- and first-floor levels were blocked by the addition of the new wing, fireplaces were included in the new south wall and an unlit cellar was added.

Hall

TO THE LEFT of the screens passage the spacious hall rises from a flagstone floor to the finely-carved timbers of its roof. Before the building's restoration this was obscured from the ground by an inserted first floor, the position of which is indicated by the mortise holes to take its joists in the face of the south-end floor beam and by the replacement of timber halfway up the aisle-posts. Other alterations to the hall include the probable

General view of the interior of the hall.

replacement of a timber partition at the northern end by a stone wall containing doorways (now blocked) which must have led through to the private apartments, and also the replacement of the central hearth by a large fireplace in the east wall. Above the

The later fireplace inserted in 1615.

fireplace arch are the arms of Hugh Gwyn bearing the date [16]15. The original floor, probably of hard-packed earth or clay, has been replaced by the present surface of old stone flags.

The roof of the hall, which is divided into two bays (the spaces between the main rafters), is best described by starting at the screens passage. Notice here that on either side of the single large truss an aisle has been formed between the posts and the wall.

Details of the aisle- or spere-truss (By kind permission of the Royal Commission on Ancient and Historical Monuments in Wales).

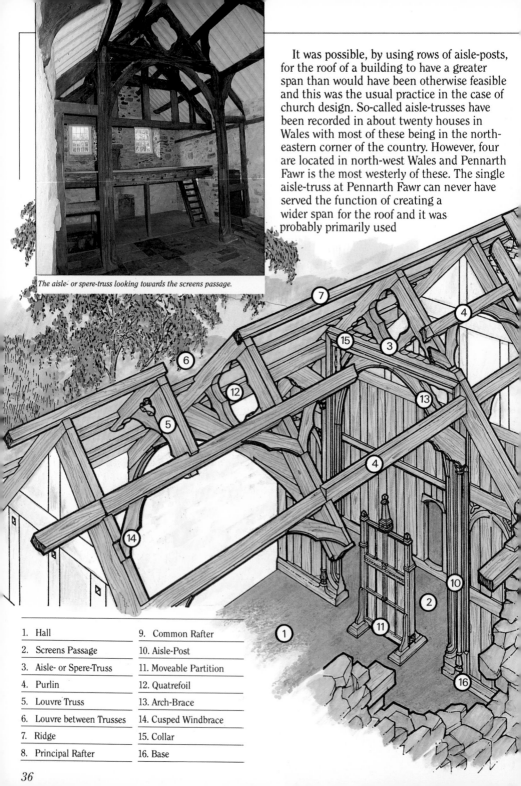

It was possible, by using rows of aisle-posts, for the roof of a building to have a greater span than would have been otherwise feasible and this was the usual practice in the case of church design. So-called aisle-trusses have been recorded in about twenty houses in Wales with most of these being in the north-eastern corner of the country. However, four are located in north-west Wales and Pennarth Fawr is the most westerly of these. The single aisle-truss at Pennarth Fawr can never have served the function of creating a wider span for the roof and it was probably primarily used

The aisle- or spere-truss looking towards the screens passage.

1. Hall	9. Common Rafter
2. Screens Passage	10. Aisle-Post
3. Aisle- or Spere-Truss	11. Moveable Partition
4. Purlin	12. Quatrefoil
5. Louvre Truss	13. Arch-Brace
6. Louvre between Trusses	14. Cusped Windbrace
7. Ridge	15. Collar
8. Principal Rafter	16. Base

for decorative effect, perhaps reflecting the status of the house's owner.

Such a single aisle-truss, forming an open division between the hall and the passage, is known as a spere-truss. A moveable partition would have been set between the two elaborately-carved posts to separate the hall from the passage. Heavy roll mouldings on

A cutaway view of the interior of the house as it might have appeared in the late fifteenth century (Illustration by Dylan Roberts).

The roof timbers of the hall looking towards the northern end of the building.

each side of the posts extend to their full height, across the collar and down the opposite post. Similar mouldings, with carved capitals and bases of late medieval type, form decorative supports for the cusped windbraces supporting the lower purlins. Other, simpler, mouldings extend up the inner side of the aisle-posts and the arch-braces supporting the collar creating a tall, carved, archway. The decoration of the truss has been further enhanced by the elaborate use of cusping which forms a quatrefoil (like a four-lobed flower) near its apex.

The central truss of the hall and the small truss just beyond it are also decorated with cusping. Together, they originally supported a louvre which would have projected above the ridge of the roof allowing smoke rising from the central hearth to escape through its sides. The plain roof truss at the northern end of the hall is similar to that on the southern side of the screens passage, although more of the original timber has survived. Here again, holes in the timbers of the truss indicate that it once had a wattle and daub infilling. As has been mentioned earlier, this does not appear to have been the original end-truss of the building which would have extended another bay to the north.

St Cybi's Well

Introduction

S T CYBI'S WELL is situated in an enchanting valley just below and to the north of Llangybi Church. It is approached by crossing a stile at the east end of the churchyard and then following a path to the far corner, across another stile, and down the side of a field into the valley.

The well is one of the most elaborate structures of its kind in this area of north Wales consisting of two well chambers, a cottage for a custodian and a small detached latrine building. The main approach is across a stone causeway on the eastern side of a low-lying waterlogged field. Another shorter causeway can be seen running from the well to the ruined remains of the latrine building.

General view of the well and cottage from the south.

Early History

T HE WELL is traditionally associated with St Cybi who is reputed to have settled in this part of Wales sometime around the middle of the sixth century A.D. Cybi is one of a group of Welsh saints whose *Lives* are to be found in a manuscript compiled around A.D. 1200. As in the case of most of the *Lives* dating to this period, that for Cybi has to be regarded as largely fictional rather than historical although a limited amount of fact is probably blended in with the myth, folklore and legend.

According to the *Life*, Cybi was born in Cornwall. He had travelled widely, particularly in the Irish Sea area, before, as a result of a dispute in Ireland, he came with his disciples to north-west Wales. Upon landing on the island of Anglesey, he is supposed to have struck a rock with his staff from which water immediately flowed.

It has been suggested that Cybi may have first landed on the Lleyn peninsula and only later moved to Anglesey. His first settlement would therefore have been here at Llangybi, which to this day bears his dedication, and

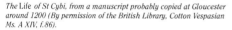

The Life of St Cybi, from a manuscript probably copied at Gloucester around 1200 (By permission of the British Library, Cotton Vespasian Ms. A XIV, f.86).

this well would have marked the spot where he struck the rock with his staff. However, in the *Life* the reference to his striking a rock is immediately preceded by the statement that Cybi had reached the island of *Monnia*. This must be Anglesey where Cybi established a monastery at Holyhead, probably within the earlier Roman fort. There is, therefore, little evidence to support an association between this well and the saint himself. The dedication probably owes its existence to his cult which was either genuinely early or, and this seems more likely, much later.

Ground Plan of the Well and Cottage

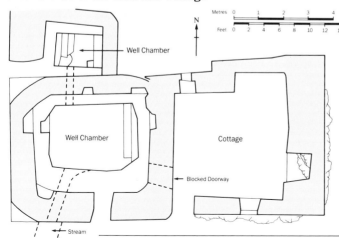

The parish church at Holyhead, within the earlier Roman fort, may be on the site of the monastery founded by St Cybi.

Later History

THE EVIDENCE for the recent history of the well is more reliable; it was a place of pilgrimage and the waters were reputed to cure warts, lameness, blindness, scrofula, scurvy and rheumatism. The well continued in use, in one form or another, after the Reformation and there was still a box, *Cyff Gybi*, for offerings in the church as late as the eighteenth century.

Dr Diederick Wessel Linden published a report in 1767 on the curative properties of the well in which he showed that the water had certain medicinal qualities. He cited twenty-eight case histories, gathered together by the Reverend Williams of Tŷ Newydd, rector of Llanystumdwy, of people who had been cured at the well over the previous twenty years or so. Seven of the thirteen cases of blindness had occurred as a result of smallpox and these seem to be the most dramatic of the cures listed. Dr Linden also noted that, 'so late as about forty years ago, several crutches, wheelbarrows, and other implements, that were used to help the decrepit to Llangybi, were hanging round this Mineral-water fountain, in testimony of their recovery'.

By the early part of the eighteenth century, the well's reputation for curing diseases had become very localized. However, Dr Linden recorded that fifteen years before his visit the Reverend Williams, having become convinced of the curative powers of the water, had persuaded the owner, William Price of Rhiwlas, of its importance and the latter had, 'caused proper conveniencies for Bathing, and other improvements to be made, at his own expence'.

Richard Fenton, when he visited Llangybi in 1813, described the well as being surrounded by a high circular wall 'coving a little at the top, but not closed'. He also referred to a declining faith in such wells.

The cottage, Tŷ'n y Ffynnon, attached to the east side of the main well chamber, may have been built for William Price. It was occupied until at least the 1870s, if not a little later, although it was uninhabitable by the turn of the century.

The well buildings were placed in State care in 1937 and they are now maintained by Cadw: Welsh Historic Monuments, on behalf of the Secretary of State for Wales.

Taking the Cure

TREATMENT APPEARS to have consisted of giving patients an equal quantity of well-water and sea-water, morning and evening, for a period varying from seven to ten days. They then had to bathe in the water once or twice a day, retiring after each bath to a bedchamber in the adjoining cottage where they were given a quantity of healing water to drink. The success or otherwise of the treatment was judged by whether the patient became warm in bed or remained cold, with the former condition indicating that the treatment was progressing satisfactorily. The patients used to throw pennies and pieces of silver into the water after each immersion and they would sometimes take bottles and casks of the water away with them.

A cutaway reconstruction of the well as it might have appeared during the second half of the eighteenth century (Illustration by Ivan Lapper).

Description

AS YOU APPROACH the well building across the stone causeway, the main well chamber is on your left with the attached cottage on the right. A narrow stone causeway leads to a small latrine building, now ruined,

General view from the south-west with the latrine building on the left.

which was probably built at the same time as the cottage. This would have been used by both patients and the occupants of the cottage with the latrine itself being located directly over the little stream, which carries water from the well chambers to the main east-west stream on the southern side of the valley.

Well Chambers

THE MAIN WELL CHAMBER is built of large blocks of stone which have the external appearance of being dry-built but which are mortared on their inner face. The two western corners (to the left) of the chamber are chamfered in all but their lowest courses and there was a similar chamfer at the north-eastern corner (back right), where the chamber is now joined to the cottage. No evidence survives to show whether the south-eastern corner was also chamfered, but the use of two very large blocks of stone to the left of the cottage doorway may point to some rebuilding in this corner.

The chamber is entered on the south side by a plain doorway and the iron stumps of the crooks for hanging the door can still be seen on the right-hand side. The chamber is roofless although the overhanging upper courses of masonry would have provided bathers with some protection from inclement weather. It is possible that it was originally intended to provide this part of the building with a corbelled roof although there is no surviving evidence to show that this was ever carried out. The main part of the chamber is occupied by the bath surrounded by a ledge

The interior of the main well chamber viewed from above.

from which steps lead down into the water on the eastern side. The water enters the bath from the north and exits on the south side. There are five niches for seats around the walls, and a narrow doorway, now blocked, in the south-eastern corner would have provided access to the adjacent cottage.

On leaving the main chamber turn to your right and go around to the back of the building where you will find the remains of another, smaller, well chamber. Here the bath is also surrounded by a ledge. Steps lead down into the water which enters on the east side and flows out into the main chamber from the south-west corner. The eastern wall is roughly bonded to the northern wall of the main chamber. To the west of both well chambers there is a roughly paved area with what may be the remains of some form of enclosure wall.

Cottage

THE COTTAGE is to the right of the main well chamber and clearly incorporates two building periods. Originally this was a single-storeyed structure with well-mortared walls and an entrance on the south side. Small round holes on the right-hand side of the doorway indicate the position of the original iron door crooks. Also on this side of the building there was a window and, in the east wall, a fireplace. The original height of the gable can still be traced on the outside face of the east end wall near the south-eastern corner.

In the second phase the walls of the building were raised to accommodate an extra floor. The cottage was also widened with a new thinner wall replacing the eastern end of the original north wall. The masonry of this work was less well mortared than that of the preceding phase as can be seen on the outside face of the wall above and to the right of the main door. All the work above the level of the first-floor window sills belongs to this period.

The east gable wall of the cottage, with the line of the roof of the earlier single-storey cottage showing near the left-hand edge of the later gable.

The remains of two roof slates from the eaves of the first building can be seen at the junction between the two phases above the door. The upper storey was lit by two windows on the south side and one, now blocked, on the east. There was also an additional fireplace at this level. A raised gable, now ruinous, on the west side of the cottage, at the junction with the eastern wall of the main well chamber, matched the surviving one to the east.

South Elevation

 Original well chamber of uncertain date
■ Mid Eighteenth Century
▨ Nineteenth Century

A nineteenth-century photograph with the northern gable wall of the cottage still standing at the junction between the main well chamber and the cottage (By courtesy of the National Library of Wales).

Well Chamber   Metres 0   1   2   3   4

Cottage

Feet 0   2   4   6   8   10   12   14

Dating

IT IS IMPROBABLE that either of the existing well chambers dates back to the sixth century. Nevertheless, a well structure, of one kind or another, could have existed on this site during the Early Christian period, or at least by the twelfth or thirteenth centuries. The present structure could date to the latter period but only if it pre-dates the cottage which would seem to be part of William Price's work of about 1750, with the extra floor probably being added sometime during the nineteenth century.

The three chamfered corners of the main well chamber pose the possibility that the south-eastern corner was also initially chamfered, thus forming a free-standing building, perhaps associated with an earlier attendant's cottage. Furthermore, the unusual appearance of the two large blocks of stone at the south-eastern corner of the well chamber suggests that this section of masonry might have been rebuilt at the same time as Price's first cottage was added. By the end of the nineteenth century the cottage was roofless.

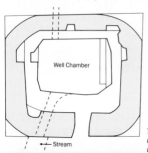

Well Chamber

Stream

Ground Plan

The possible early arrangement of the main well chamber.

Metres 0   1   2
Feet 0   2 4 6 8

The chamfered south-western corner of the main well chamber.

Further Reading

The following books and articles form the principal sources consulted during the preparation of this guide.

Criccieth Castle
R. Avent, *Cestyll Tywysogion Gwynedd / Castles of the Princes of Gwynedd* (HMSO, Cardiff 1983), 17-25, 31.
C.A. Gresham, 'The Development of Criccieth Castle', *Transactions of the Caernarvonshire Historical Society,* **34** (1973), 14-22.
C.A. Gresham, *Eifionydd* (Cardiff 1973), 169-71.
An Inventory of the Ancient and Historical Monuments in Caernarvonshire, Vol. 2, *Central* (RCAHM Wales, London 1960), 59-62.
C.N. Johns, *Criccieth Castle* (HMSO, London 1970).
B.H. St J. O'Neil, 'Criccieth Castle, Caernarvonshire', *Archaeologia Cambrensis,* **98** (1944-45), 1-51.
A. Taylor, *The Welsh Castles of Edward I* (London 1986), 73-75, 117-19.
D. Turnbull, 'Some Problems about the Origin of Criccieth Castle', *Fort,* **7** (1979), 52-68.

Pennarth Fawr
C.A. Gresham, *Eifionydd* (Cardiff 1973), 269-76.
An Inventory of the Ancient and Historical Monuments in Caernarvonshire, Vol. 3, *West* (RCAHM Wales, London 1964), 112-13.
P. Smith, *Houses of the Welsh Countryside,* 2nd ed (HMSO London 1988), 96-9, 113a-b, 124.

St Cybi's Well
R. Avent, *St Cybi's Well/Ffynnon Gybi* (HMSO, London 1982).
An Inventory of the Ancient and Historical Monuments in Caernarvonshire, Vol. 2, *Central* (RCAHM Wales, London 1960), 205-06.
An Inventory of the Ancient and Historical Monuments in Caernarvonshire, Vol. 3, *West* (RCAHM Wales, London 1964), 121-22.
D.W. Linden, *Enquiry into the Properties of the Mineral Water of Llangybi, in Carnarvonshire* (London 1767).
W. Williams, 'Some Traces and Traditions Round Llangybi', *Archaeologia Cambrensis 6 series,* **4** (1904), 107-18.